CW01369176

Moored Man

Moored Man

POEMS OF NORTH NORFOLK

Kevin Crossley-Holland

WATERCOLOURS & ETCHINGS

Norman Ackroyd

ENITHARMON EDITIONS

First published in 2006 by
Enitharmon Editions
26B Caversham Road
London NW5 2DU

ISBN 1 904634 52 4 (*de luxe*)
1 904634 53 2 (regular)

Contents

List of Illustrations

* The asterisked images are taken from sketchbooks used on visits to Norfolk in 2003–2004

Moored Man

Much of the north Norfolk coast is a mesh of saltmarshes, tidal creeks, sand dunes, sand-flats and shingle ridges. It is dramatic, complex, and in flux.

Moored Man is the spirit of this wild place, and he embodies its warring elements. He moulds the dykes and sorts and carts gravel; he eats jetties and groynes, and dredges and infills creeks, tricks and cuts off the unwary, drowns children, howls like the wind and dances like the sea, and each day destabilises himself. Seen from a human viewpoint, some of his actions are constructive, some destructive, some apparently meaningless; all are repetitive.

Although Moored Man is no thinker, he keeps trying to work out who he is and where he has come from. Was he always only male? Could he once swim? And fly? What is his relationship to seal and seabird? Human beings largely ignore or abuse him, but he is by turns deeply attracted to them and savagely angry with them, and he constantly tries to undermine their plans and management.

Like the coastline itself, Moored Man is virile; he keeps changing (among his forms are those of trickster and shape-changer); he suffers; he endures; and he has a fierce beauty. In a sense, the poems are a set of enquiries into a causal and contradictory identity.

Moored Man's Song

His feet are caked with creek mud,
his shins are indigo.

And yet Moored Man lifts his eyes
across the slakes, across the waste
and sees an island, riding.

His arms are tied with marram roots,
his thighs strapped with green weed.
He wears a fraying halter.

Moored Man lifts his grey eyes
and peers through iron-cold bars.

Colours of salt and honey.

He is half-old, tide-worn, wind-worn.
He roars and starts to sing.

Moored Man Almost Remembers

Sheen-eyed and unblinking, quick
to the creek's sudden lurches and quivers.

Undergrowling
at the far fierce crash and pound
deep day makes sullen.

Before all this.

Did he fall?

Was it a hundred wings with one will
raised him into air-tides?
When he swam and drifted. When he cried.

At dawn he rises from the groyne
under the barefaced sky.
His forearms shine and ripple.

Once more he braces his blunt thumbs
and sinks them into boulders.

One blue window in his mind.
One feather tarred to his left shoulder.

Making the Island

Why?
Because it welled up – a single keen wave
out of the flatcalm of his mind.

He squelched and splashed north.
He waded out
a mile and more
up to his thighs, his hips.

Why?
To see felicity.

On the hazy bar he began.
With both feet he scratched and scraped
like a wild sea-cat covering its faeces,
until his ankles were bloody and raw.

Then he kicked. He kicked.

Why?
So the Polar reach
would end in his ears.

The gravel flew and dropped,
it swarmed and swirled like chaff
in the murky water.

Longshore drift did the rest.
Pebbles and grit swam
and settled in new stations.
They rose above themselves
out of the water.

Schschschhh-huh!
Soft echoes in the cavern of his mouth.

Time and wind.

A shining cap of sand!
Sea-kale, tugging at its roots.
Sea-holly, growing beautiful
as it grows old.

Sss-sk!   Sss-sk!
He strikes sounds on his sandpaper tongue.
Sss-sk! Tt! Tt!

The sun draws its blade
over his welling land.

Why?
Because it was not there.

He stares at his island
and knows he is beautiful.

HOLKAM.

Young Woman

He begins with her toes.
One by one
by one he massages them
and paints them silver-blue.

He applies indigo poultices
to her porcelain ankles.

Then he shows her his claws.
Scratches her shins all over, very lightly,
until she stands shivering under midday sun.

And kneels to him.

The further she comes
the more he grows towards her
and reaches out behind her.

The backs of her knees:
he tickles them with a feathery wisp.
And then he wraps himself around her skinny thighs:
bleached pink, lavender.

He is waiting for her at the hanging valley
and the dark pool.

She stares at herself in him.

Instead of a Roar

First he sees everything, then
narrows his gaze
to nothing but his fierce intention.

Three lolloping, laughing boys,
each blowing mist balloons
and stuffing them with loud words.
The point of his silence lies in wait for them.

Next, the retriever walking his chapped mistress
baring his teeth and grinning:
for one the slip,
slime and mud-slurp for the other.

High on the dyke's shoulder
black pods rattle
and late bugs trundle over lank grasses.
The parcelled woman with sore eyelids
stumbles, sobs.
Wasteland of my heart, she thinks.

He is like the barn owl:
pouring out of himself upwards
and very fast, quietly
spreading the dark sheet of his shadow.

One disciple stands his ground.
He watches Moored Man for months; for years;
He sees through him.

Foreigners

Where are they always going?
Why are they coloured yesterday and tomorrow?
Foreigners!
Why do they have so little to do with him?

They goggle at him through binoculars
and chuck empties at him.
They swear at him and shit on him
because they cannot see him.

Moored Man is still glad, though.
He likes how they look,
and their looking at each other.

He likes his dreams.

When dark clouds laced with silver
gang round the sun
and shadow-ribs race away across the marsh
into the mudflats,

he sobs inside himself again,
unblinded and knowing
how they must have to do with him.

Waste

When they hurry through, eyes cockleshelled
against the savage light,
declaring they love him and what would they do
without him,

and how all summer
he was benelsoned
like Lady Hamilton's breasts,

and how his groynes
need more attention

their words are only for themselves
and each other.

His heart aches.
His ears start to sing.

He watches three curlews work sobbing water.
He inspects the massive spar
dressed in stars of salt
with rot in its gut.

His bones – are they melting?
One day he feels almost weightless,
the next he sinks back blue
into himself,

and he broods
until the tide turns in him once more
and he could rise and ramp
before the howling wind
and blot out everything.

Unknowing

Pear and pale pink and oatmeal
 – he can see for miles
the southern rim breaking
into colour,
flaunting spring flags.

He can hear the taunts of golden trumpets,
and the piercing cries of children,
and young lovers sighing in their bones.

So pitted and pocked.
So invaded. So exhausted.
What is he
today but an old grey map again
crossing itself?

Moored Man grinds his heels. His teeth.
He cannot help himself.

He stamps
and his mud splatters the sky's pane.

He thumb-stops his ears.
Crouching, he sees nothing
for hailshot, for hot tears.

Moored Man's Plan

He sleeps with a stone on his stomach.
When he wakes
he sees the upshot waiting for him:

crabs will sidle from their shells,
lobster pots turn themselves inside out,
mussels will play their castanets;
buoys will harness themselves in weeds,
saltwater and freshwater
will stand up and embrace.

What a dance!
Snub-noses bucking, clinkers slipping anchor.
The price of disrespect.

First he must cock his ears.
He must listen
deep into the sound
of the sound where all sounds meet.

Next he must make of his own throat
and diaphragm a winding marsh-horn.

Moored Man's yawn: it is whale-wide.

The third thing. The third
will be the third thing
will . . .

Whale-wide; cloud-wide.
Again he falls asleep.

His Voice

Growling as he sleeps,
his own sinking world's ground-bass.

His voice is like the memory
of gunnery practice out at sea.

Dark brother
of the swill and pound and chatter
way beyond the cockle bight,

ocean's mouth
ancient and still promising
to deceive.

Witness

While he peels off his tatters, sodden
with dew, and tosses them into sky,

his tern flaps and hovers,
its javelin scream
white as the edge of the first morning.

What does he see?
A looming impression
in the creek's murky obsidian
and the flashy mudflats?

Can he see himself at all
in the green shoots bristling on the marsh,
the leprous rashes of sea-pink?

They see him.
They bear witness to him.

Naked he stands,
upright
where restless levels meet:

tall as a sun-lance,
a bright column striking,

while on an air-stream
his tern balances.

Ablutions

He begins to stretch through himself
– his daily becoming.

Sharp blue teeth; flounders and flatfeet;
sudden sloshing.
Then the crook-necked grey one
stabbing and gulping.

He stares at his skin's asterisks –
salt-crusted scars,
spatters of flowers like service-medals –
and lets each tide rinse through him.

Once again the ruckled beds and lays
go under, and the soft mound, silver and grey,
around the freshwater spring.

Each day he rises,

and over his head
the light grows fearsome.

Trickster

As though he were the son
of apparent light and the mimic jay:

he quivers and glares,
he unrolls carpets of sticky mud,
then spits laughter as he laces
fine sand with pointed stones.

And as though he were screaming quicksilver:

he rises to the moon,
drags the lumpen tides
until the creek's swollen and impassable . . .

But tricksters turn to darkness.

He licks oozing blood,
rubs salt into wounds;
he cracks and snaps bones.
In the evening he drowns little children,
and then he howls with remorse.

Old and wild and angry,
child of mayhem,
father of grief.

The Same Badge

When they inhale his minerals, their blood
fizzes. They soon grow giddy.

Standing on a mudslide spit
a young leftie casts his line, slips
and barbs his own right thumb.

Their slates are too good to lose.
Two boys playing ducks-and-drakes
skim them across the narrow creek
straight at one another's shins.

Now someone's daughter leaps
from Old Stoker's wreck,
drives her incisors through her lower lip.

Each summer victim wears his badge:
a ring of stinging iodine
around the leaking wound's mouth.

Before the Storm

What is on its way, massing
upstream, is like a tower about to topple
or a cloak of spelter bruised with purple.

And what is smooth-ironing
the afternoon's long sleeve
is his own stillness. Effortless his water
swans down midstream, softly
it backheels in the margins.

Each minute hangs and seeps. It trickles
through his myriad gorges of mud.

Birds cross very high, out of earshot,
and balls of gnats ferment
while still he dozes,
one glassy eye open,
until his sheer shine could blind you.

Storm's gonfalons hoisted and advancing,
Moored Man unhurried but at bay:
this perfect equilibrium
arrested
on the shield of the waiting day.

His Shadow, His Smile

When her own quicksands
snagged the woman on the foreshore
and, choking, she did all she could
to clutch her left breast,

Moored Man trembled until
his bone-joints cracked. His teeth ached.

Laser gulls tacked into the headwind,
shrouds and halyards keened;
low he stooped
and threw his long shadow over her.

Stopgo shrimps soon sized her up.
Come whiskers, come pincers!
Come terns and cormorants!

She was his golden cornstook,
she was his wave-cornflower
until the jade tide turned and made,
and beckoned her.

Gently Moored Man smiled
as the pale sun blinks and smiles
on the stranded and the breathless,
on the dark wave's welling
and winter wheat.

Searching for the Stone

On seventh days
his labour is to search for the stone.

He turns his back on the comfortable bells,
the silk-and-velvet cattle
stamping on each other's shadows.
First to comb the foreshore after high water.

Although it is there
it is never there
at first, and then as no more than a glint
in the corner of his bloodshot eye.
He rakes the shingle beds beside the creek,
glares until each stone turns sepia.
Until pebbles crunch his brains.

And then
it is there.

Utter,
transparent and unblinking.

Between his rough fingers he holds it up.
He raises it,
free and shining,
quite clear of time.

But he knows what he has to do:
he draws back his arm,
hurls it, slings it
into the water's throat,
as far from him as it has always been.

Moored Man's Tides

He faces the offing and world's rim.
Home of the nightfall.

This bickering and sucking soft, this
lapping as tide grows heavy in itself,
then dies to be reborn:

how does it mean? How do tides mean?
This falling and rising,
moaning and thrust.

In his gut the puzzle bubbles and ferments
but still cannot surface.

If only he could spring it –

the welter; the rim;
the colours of separation;
always the ache of his tides
chiming
deep within.

Her in Him

He sees how she spreads herself.

The scallops of her palms,
the little blue hollows.
Her ribs – their pale crescents and sparkle –
and the clippings of pearly razor-shells.

Her salt-stiffened sprays of green hair.

Ankle-whip, shin-whip:
she wears skirts of wild silk
slit to the thighs.

Soft, stale O of the hagstone's mouth.

Each night the cold white flames
of the slakes and oozing meals.

Ghost-Light

Under the Milky Way
his hidden lips and little throats
open, they stay open
as he sips and gurgles.

Under the dark, burning spaces
he spreads himself and plots himself.
Prone and accepting.

He strops his blades
under the red star.
Like nerves his wiry hairs quiver.

Under the wrenching moon
he is slats of ghost-light,
he is ribs and rising.
All he is, all he was
in this dream of re-becoming.

Quite

No one knows.

Or, rather, everyone knows
but each tells a quite different tale.

Moored Man listens.
He sleeps with one eye open,
gauzy with death-mist.
He who hears the artillery
of popping bubbles, beetles tap-dancing
and the shooting scooters,
listens.

They were home on leave.
They were Home Guards.
Foreigners.
They were Germans.

Both men were wearing identical uniforms.
At Bank Hole, beside the groyne,
they stripped, or did not strip
but the sea stripped them, naked.

It’s a day’s dive to the bottom.
Diz with her webbed fingers and webbed feet
is the only one who ever touched it,

unless they touched it.
When the whirlpool dragged them down.

What of their stigmata?
Snagged, gashed on a spar's nails.
No! Drowned men split and tear.
No! They clawed each other.

Moored Man listens
until they are quite finished.

All everyone agrees
is both men were found floating,
they were lolling
side by side, moon-faces up.

Morston Creek March 04

Saying

Saying:

I had forgotten as the old forget
this morning's deep charge:

plumbing each orifice,
gouging scum from my veins,
bursting my pockets.

All my pus and jetsam!
I will usher it
into the marsh
where now filters into then.

Saying:

I turn, I make, I flow, I come.
I also am young.

His Line

Headline. Heartline.

Line from once to will be.
Innocence to responsibility.

His skyline
murmuring
to west, to east.

His line about you
and now
if not always.

Marooned Man

Is this it?

Nothing barking; or breaking;
no chitter-chatter.
Nothing in the spire-shells of his ears.

Amongst the reeds of the freshwater creek
the chugging coots make not a sound;
neither does the sizzle of gnats.

He is cocooned and cannot see himself
in focus, only that he's dressed
in shining, sticky webs.

The gut's half-drained and listless.
His limbs are limp.
Nothing's bated.

Is this how it will be
– this erosion of the senses, this exhaustion,
one long ooze?

His skin is drenched,
his arms outstretched.

Yet he is smiling almost,
still alive, marooned, and unfree.

Norfolk - Flood Tide

Moored Man
has been designed at
Libanus Press, Marlborough.
The text is set in Collis
and printed on 170 gsm Mega Matt by BAS Printers.

The *de luxe* edition, slipcased by
The Fine Bindery, consists of ninety copies
and twenty-five *hors commerce* copies, signed by the
poet and artist and numbered 1 to 90 and i to xxv.
With each copy is a signed and numbered
original etching by Norman Ackroyd RA,
printed on Somerset 280 gsm antique rag.

The regular edition consists of
1,500 hardback copies.